Go Pro Camera
Video Editing for Beginners

How to Edit Video
in Final Cut Pro and Adobe Premiere Pro
Step by Step

Vlad Gemstone

CONTENTS

ABOUT THE AUTHOR

I am a young, aspiring author. I love travelling, healthy lifestyle and meditation. I am also interested in spirituality, yoga practices, Advaita tradition, the ancient knowledge of different peoples. I enjoy riding a bike or elektroskooter. I do not drink or smoke and I have not eaten meat for more than 4 years. I am happily married with several children. I love the beauty of nature more than objects created by human hands. I do not trust radio or television, and I do not want to waste my precious time with them. I do not trust modern medicine. Ayurveda students apply their knowledge for a happy life with good results I have written several books on topics related to computer technology, healthy lifestyle and alternative medicine. They will appear here when they are released. I may soon write books on the subject of my personal travel to Asia.

1 GOPRO: INTRODUCTION

If you are one of those people who never miss an opportunity to see the world then, at some point, you must have needed a camera to capture a specific moment. There are many moments in our lives which are so special that we want to keep reliving those moments or we simply want to share those amazing moments with our friends and family. For these kinds of people, GoPro camera is a must. Now if you aren't familiar with the name GoPro, which is highly unlikely, then don't worry. After reading this book you will be familiar with what a GoPro camera is and almost everything about it which includes the way it works and various software's to make the best out of it.

GoPro is basically an American corporation, with headquarters in California, which is known to manufacture high quality personal cameras for everyone. The company was founded by Nick Woodman in 2002 and they are dominating the world of digital photography and film making since they released their first camera in 2004. GoPro has a comprehensive range of cameras with various features to suit all types of users whether they are entry level photographers, amateurs or professionals. Their cameras are known to be small and compact yet efficient at the same time. GoPro cameras are widely used for personal use because of the fact that they aren't just specifically designed for photography professionals, with lots of complex features. Rather they are simple to use and light to carry which makes them perfect scene-capturing gadgets for every individual who likes to keep memories of their best moments.

You can use GoPro cameras for anything you want. Whether you are going for surfing, sightseeing, traveling or attending a major event, a GoPro camera is a must-have because you can capture high quality pictures as well as make high resolution videos which would be quite difficult without a GoPro HD camera at your disposal. GoPro cameras come with an amazing set of accessories to ease your way of capturing the best moments of your life. The list of accessories is quite a long one which includes a 3-way mount, clamp, suction cup and many more. Along with the accessories, you can use their video editing software or any other third party video editing software which can help you refine or edit your videos.☐

You can find a list of products that GoPro offers to its customers in their stores. It might be confusing for a person, who doesn't know a lot about cameras or specifically about GoPro products, as to what product suits them the best. Well, the most recent and most advanced GoPro product is the HERO 4 which is responsible for one of the best and stunning videos that you can find out there on the internet. GoPro HERO 4 has 2 editions: GoPro HERO 4 Black edition and GoPro HERO 4 Silver edition. There are a few differences in both of these editions which we will describe in the next chapter. Their latest products offer one of the best video quality and the most powerful photo-capturing tools in the market. GoPro HERO 4 was released in September of 2014.

Before releasing GoPro HERO 4, GoPro HERO 3+ was the leading product in the market. GoPro HERO 3+ also had a Black edition and a Silver edition. These are the two top products of GoPro that are dominating the market these days. Of course, there are many other products that GoPro puts on the table like GoPro HERO 3 and many other camera models, mounts, accessories, software's and many more which can be surfed through their official website gopro.com.

Now that you know a little bit about GoPro and what its top products are, we will cover all the features of its top products in detail in the upcoming chapter. After a complete introduction to all the products and features of GoPro cameras, we will get you familiarized with the video editing software's that can be used to make your captured moments a lot more amazing than before.

2 GOPRO LATEST CAMERAS

As mentioned in the previous chapter, GoPro has a comprehensive range of products to satisfy all its customers. Whether you are a professional who wants top-of-the-line HD camera or you're just an amateur who's looking for a budget camera to capture the best moments of his/her vacations, GoPro cameras will be available to meet all kinds of requirements.□

GoPro's latest and the most advanced camera is HERO 4 which was just released at the end of 2014. The HERO 4 has Silver and a Black edition. One of the main differences of GoPro HERO 4 from its predecessors is its new processor that GoPro claims to be twice as fast as the previous HERO 3+ camera models. A processor with double the speed of its previous processor will definitely make the frame rate of almost everything. This is quite an accomplishment which will make a huge difference in the performance of GoPro HERO 4. GoPro HERO 4 also includes several connectivity features like Bluetooth and Wi-Fi which makes it a lot easier to transfer your data from one device to another without so much effort.

GoPro HERO 4 (Black Edition) can capture a maximum of 12MP stills with 30 fps and records 4k videos at 25 as well as 30 fps but other resolutions and rates are also available with this camera model.

The overall performance of the device isn't much different from its predecessor GoPro HERO 3+ at close range.

However GoPro HERO 4 beats all its predecessors by delivering much more detailed long ranged recordings. Upon making a 4K/30 fps videos, the batteries of GoPro HERO 4 usually last 65 minutes without any wireless connectivity like Wi-Fi. On the other hand battery timings are extended up to 1 hour and 50 minutes at 720/120 recordings. GoPro HERO 4 Silver edition has nothing in common with GoPro HERO 4 Black edition except the options of wireless connectivity like Wi-Fi and Bluetooth. GoPro HERO 4 Silver edition has all the specs of GoPro HERO 3+ with an addition of a touch screen.

Upon buying a camera from a GoPro outlet you will get a wide range accessories as well as a copy of their video editing software as well. Although there video editing software works fine but using third party video editing software is more beneficial. Third party software comes with a lot more functionality and lots of extra plug-ins. Also, third party video editing software will provide support for lots of platforms. In the next couple of chapters we will discuss some of the most widely used video editing programs to get you started with video editing. Video editing is an essential skill to learn if you are planning on buying a GoPro camera.

3 FINAL CUT PRO (X): YOUR FIRST VIDEO EDITING TUTORIAL

Final Cut Pro (X) is one of the most widely used video editing software. Using Final Cut Pro (X) to edit your GoPro videos will be the best idea. If you are new to video editing software and don't know much about video editing then worry not. At the end of this chapter you will be familiar with not all but most of the basic concepts of video editing.

First of all you need to know all about the windows of the Final Cut Pro (X) and get familiar with its interface so you don't have any difficulty in finding the right windows and buttons during video editing. Upon opening your Final Cut Pro (X) you will be looking at blank video editing software with lots of windows.

Go Pro Camera: Video Editing for Beginners

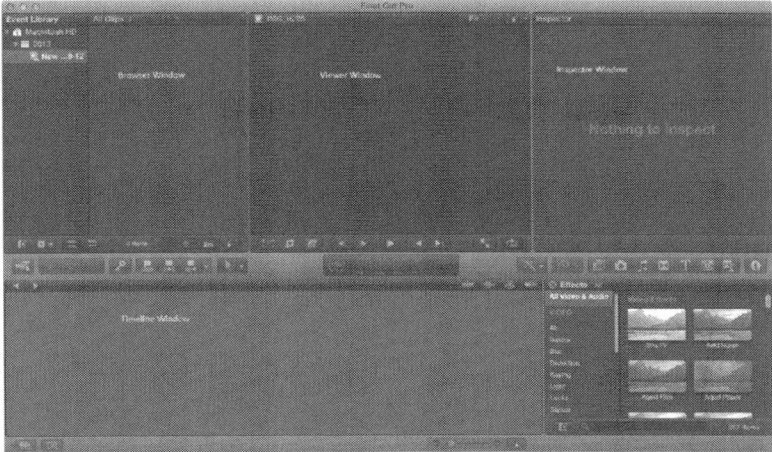

4 LIBRARIES, EVENTS AND BROWSER WINDOW

You will find a window named "Libraries" on the left-most side of your video editing software. This window is used for making libraries and events. An event is simply a sequence of multiple clips that you will find in your browser window which we will discuss in a while. You can have multiple events in a single library which means that you will be able to store many sequences in your Final Cut Pro (X) software. Just on the right side of your libraries you will find a window named as browser window. This window is responsible for collecting and organizing all of your imported videos. Basically whatever you import inside your Final Cut Pro (X) it will be imported directly to your browser window from where you will be doing all the editing and moving of those clips etc.

5 VIEWER AND INSPECTOR WINDOW

Just on the right side of your browser window, you will find the viewer window. This window will be showing you your clips and edited movies. Basically this window is used to watch your edited as well as unedited clips. Also, the marking of videos, which we will discuss later in this chapter, will be done here as well. You can think of this video as a viewing window which lets you play your videos so you can see whether or not you like your editing. Just on the right side of your viewer's window you will find the inspectors window which will assist you in changing the properties of your clips. You will be able to see all the properties of your selected clips inside this window. You will find three tabs in inspector window namely Video, Audio and Info. You can change the color and other properties related to appearance in Video tab and you can turn on and off the audio tracks from Audio tab. Info tab can be used to get the properties and other information about your selected clips.

6 TIME LINE WINDOW AND STORYLINE

The long window on the bottom of your Final Cut Pro (X) is known as the timeline window. This window will contain your edited video. Your timeline window contains a dark black line in the middle of the window and grey parts right above or below the black part. The edited parts of your clips, for example trimmed and edited parts, will be brought in this window's storyline. A storyline is basically the name of your current video that you're working on. For example if you just brought in a trimmed clip inside your timeline window it will be added to your storyline and you will be able to see a clip sitting in the dark black area of your timeline window. If you bring in another short clip, it will be added to your storyline just after your first clip (there are ways to add your clips on desired points of your storyline which we will discuss in a while). This way you can make your storyline by bringing in videos with effects. When, at the end, you export your edited video, all of your storyline containing all your edited and merged clips is what you will get.

7 TRIMMING AND ADDING CLIPS TO YOUR STORYLINE

Now that you know the basics of Final Cut Pro (X) windows and what their functions are, now it's time to understand the basics of editing a video in Final Cut Pro (X).

• The very first thing you need to do in order to edit a video is import video clips so you can either merge or edit them and make a new clip from them.

• First make a library and make a new event. Keep in mind that an event is a sequence of clips so all your imported clips will be in your event. An event can also be thought of as a simple folder. Also, make a new project inside your timeline window so you don't have to make it later. There will be an icon appearing in your timeline window saying make a new project. Just simply click that icon.

• Now you need to import some video clips which you can do by going to Files > Import and then select the files you want to import to your browser window.

• Since your browser window is responsible for holding all the original clips you will be able to see all your imported videos inside this window. You can hover your mouse on these videos that are inside your browser window and they will appear in your viewer's window. You can then either press space or click on the play button appearing in your viewer's window to play those videos.

•   Trimming is an essential part of video editing process because most of the videos are very long which is quite boring. So most of the time during your video editing process you will be adding effects as well as trimming your original clips at the same time. In order to clip your original videos drag your mouse on the clip that you want to trim and click on the part from where you want your trimmed part to start. In the viewers window you will be able to see the exact part of the video that you have selected. If the selected point is satisfying for you then press "I" to make it your input point which means that it will be your starting point. Now click on your video clip again to select an output point which will tell your software where to stop trimming. If your clicked point is appropriate then press "o" to make it your output point; otherwise you can keep choosing the points in your video until you find the right spot.

• Now press w or select the button on your toolbar, just below your browser window, that says click to insert into storyline.

• Using the same technique of trimming you can trim as many video clips as you want and press w to put them in your storyline. Now where your newest edited clip goes into the storyline is completely dependent on you. Originally, there will be a line or a head point in your storyline which will act as a pivot point for your newest added video meaning that your newest added video will be inserted at the point in your storyline where your play head is. On the other hand if you don't want to move your play head every time you add a new clip to your storyline you can press e or press the button in your toolbar that says append. You will find this button adjacent to the button that you used to add clips to your storyline.

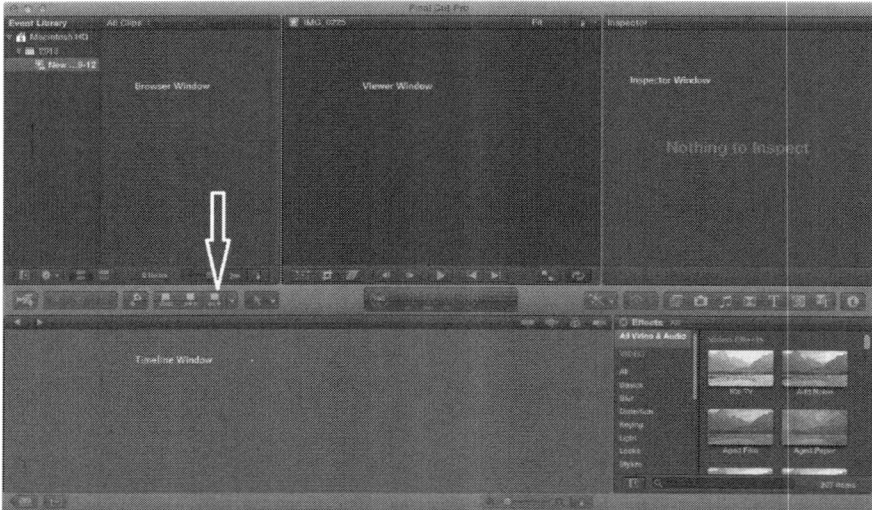

8 ADDING MUSIC TO YOUR STORYLINE

You can play your storyline video right from your timeline to get an idea of your edited video. However, sometimes the background noise or audio of the original video is undesirable. So if you want to add some music or remove the audio from your storyline clips just simply select the clips from your storyline and go to your inspector window, select the Audio tab and then go to Channel Configuration and deselect the audio.

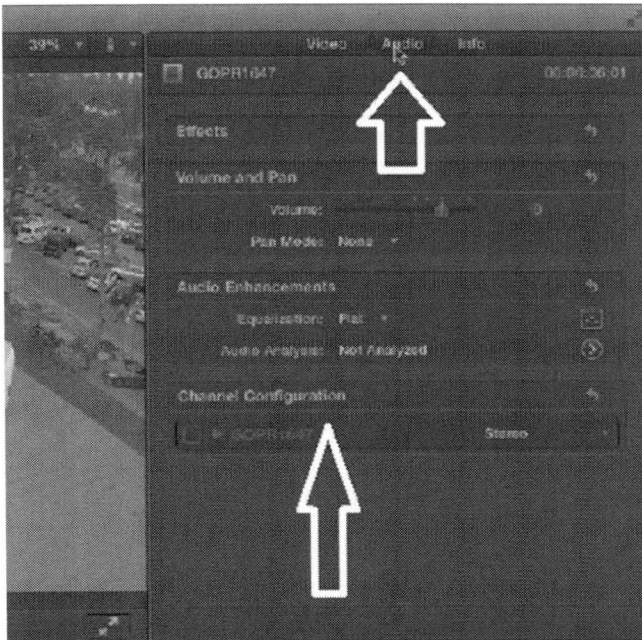

In Final Cut Pro (X), music is considered as media so you need to add new music files the same way you imported your video files into your browser window because you have to add music or audio to your clips in storyline. After importing your music clip just simply select the music clip from your browser window and press q which will add the music clip to your storyline without disturbing it. You can also use the button on the left side of 'add to storyline' button in your toolbar.

9 TRANSITIONS AND EFFECTS

Transitioning and other effects are a major part of video editing. Video editing isn't all about trimming and joining the right kind of clips all together. You have to make a lot of changes in appearance as well as in background music of the video to make it a good one.

☐

To add transitioning effects like fade in and fade out to your music simply go to the end of your music track in your storyline. Here, hover your mouse pointer at the edge of your track and you will see your pointer change into a new symbol with arrows on left and right. If you hover your mouse at the key frame for a long time you will see a text saying audio fade out or in depending on the edge of the track you're on. When your pointer changes shape then click and drag your mouse left or right for fade out and fade in respectively.

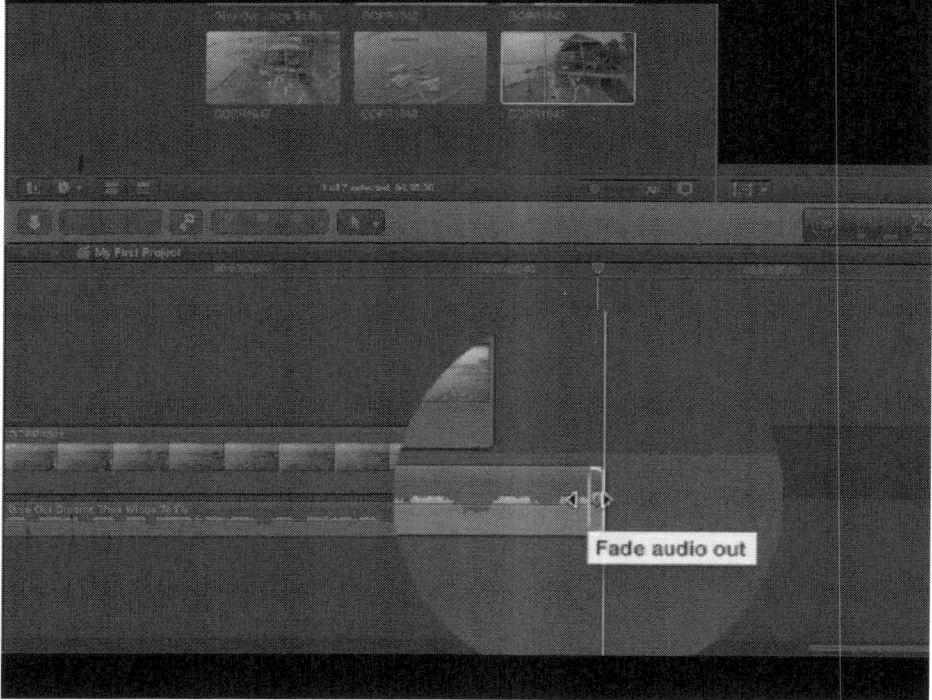

Fade audio out

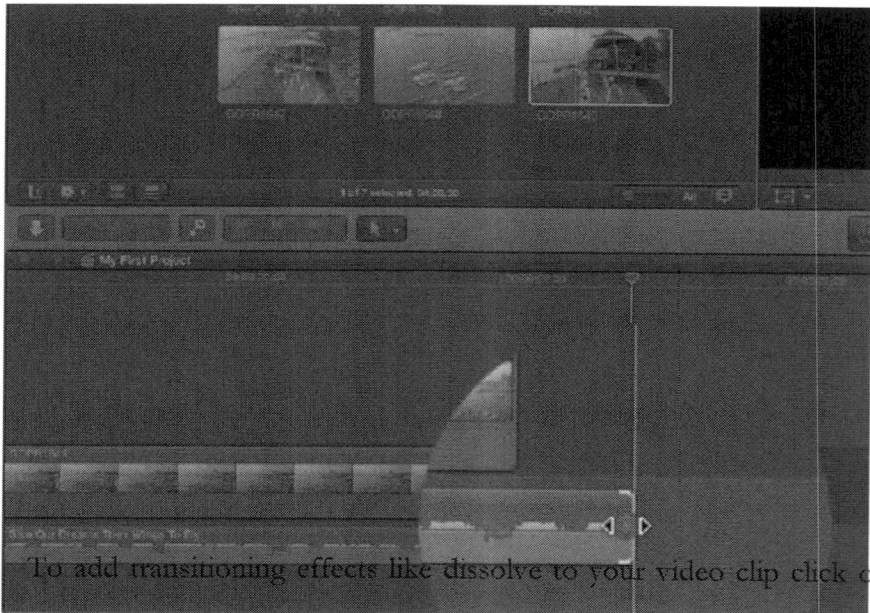

To add transitioning effects like dissolve to your video clip click on

18

the transitions browser button which can be found on the right side of the toolbar just above your timeline window. In the transition browser you will find all sorts of transitioning effects for your video. Just select the one you want for your video and drag it to the end or start of a clip. It's worth noting that transitioning effects can only be added between two different clips or at the start and end of a clip.

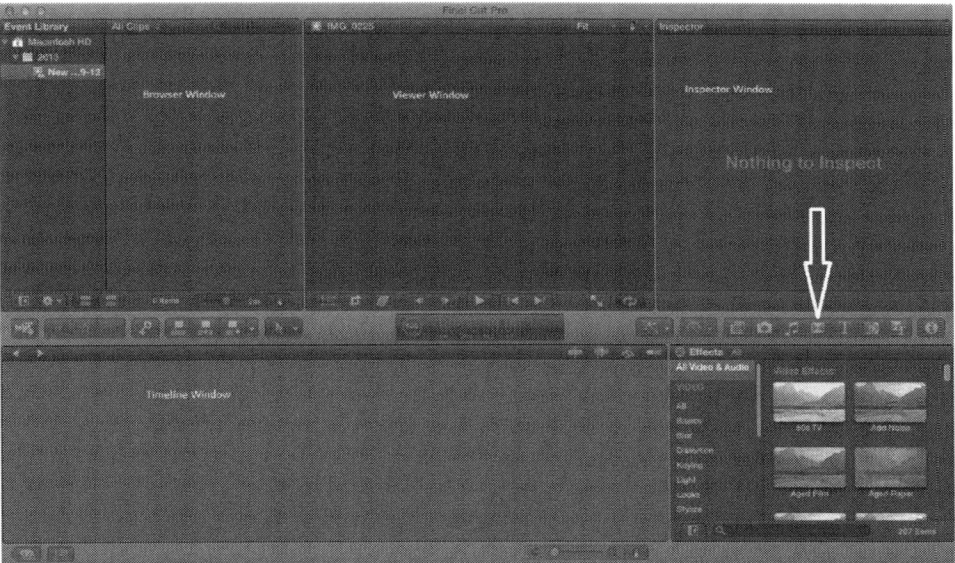

10 EXPORT OR SHARE

Upon completing your storyline, you would like to export your video so you can share it with your friends and family. In Final Cut Pro (X) exporting is known as sharing. So if you look for an export button then you won't find it.

You will find your share button on the right-most side of the toolbar that resides right in the middle of your screen. Click on your share button and select the platform you want to share your video with. Select the option "Add Destination" and a new window will open which will show you different ways of sharing your file. You can also choose a destination of your own by clicking on the "Export File" option from the newly popped-up window. Now you can change the name of your video by clicking on it (just like you rename any file). Select the format of your video e.g.

□ Video only, audio only etc. and select a video type. One of the most popular video types is H.264; so choose that if you're not sure about other types. Once you're done, close the window.

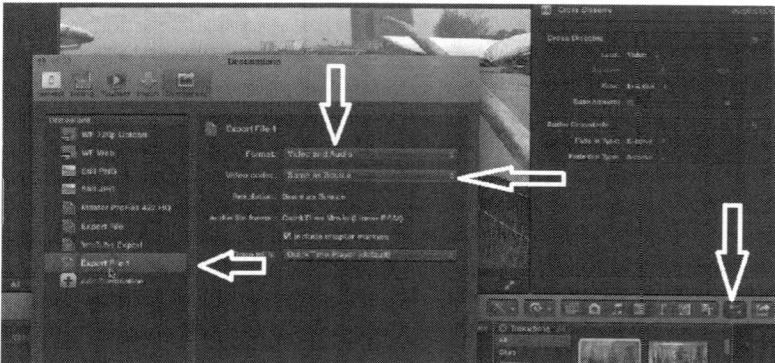

Select your share button again and now you will see the name of your file appearing in the share button menu. Click on your file name and it will open a new window for you with the properties of your file like fps and resolution. You can change the settings by clicking on the "Settings" tab. After you are done with changing the settings then click "Next" and choose the destination of your file then click "Save".

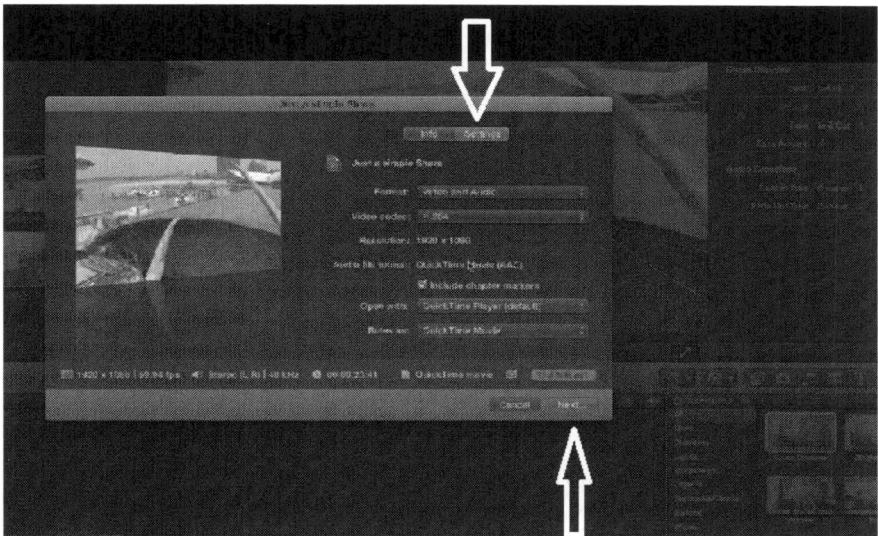

Now you're done with editing your file and you can use it for anything you want. The above mentioned features of Final Cut Pro (X) will be used in almost every video editing process so make sure to follow all the steps mentioned. In the next chapter you will do almost the same basic editing in video editing software called Adobe Premiere Pro.

11 VIDEO EDITING IN ADOBE PREMIERE PRO

Adobe Premiere Pro is another top of the line video editing software. This software can be used to edit as well as make new videos from different original ones without so much effort. In this chapter you will learn the basics of video editing. You must be wondering you just learnt basics of video editing in the previous chapter so why would you want to learn them again?

The answer of this question is that different third party video editing tools have different interfaces and, therefore, different methods to do the same thing. In this chapter you will be doing the same things but with a little bit of difference.

12 MAKING PROJECT

First you need to make a project so you can add your assets and save edited files. To make a project open Adobe Premiere Pro and click create new project on the welcome screen. You might have noticed that there are many more options to choose from as well from this new project window but leave them as it is for now.

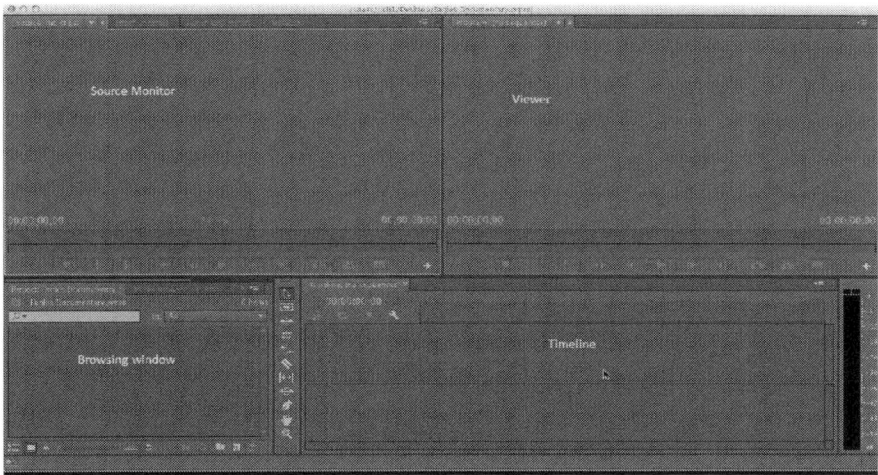

13 IMPORTING

Pictures, video clips, music clips and other graphics are an option for you when it comes to importing your assets.

In the bottom left corner of your screen you will find a window with a media file browser tab where you will be able to import your assets. Bins are basically folders which can be used for organizing your assets in whatever way you want.

You can browse your available hard drives from your media file browser to pick the folder containing your assets. When you are finished with importing your assets you can click on the projects tab, in the same window, to see your imported assets and make bins for your assets.

14 SEQUENCES

You can make sequences for your project from the assets that you imported earlier. You can think of sequences or timelines as a sequence of your clips in a manner over time. The clips, however, will be in an arranged way.

As mentioned earlier, sequences are made up of video clips or assets. So to make a sequence open your bin in project tab and select a video clip that you want to be a part of your sequence. Double clicking your desired video clip will make it appear in the source monitor (a window right above your project tab).

Your source monitor will show you the starting point of your shot that will be used to make your sequence. You can play your video clip in your source monitor if you like to watch the video first.

Now it's time to cut your original video, the video in your source monitor, so you can add a piece of your video to the timeline. You can definitely use your entire clip in your timeline but usually there are many unwanted parts in clips that you don't want to appear in your new video. □

To cut your video you can use your play head to select the starting point of your video by clicking on the "in" button right below your source monitor window. Now you need to select an "out" point which will be used as an ending point for your trimmed video. Use your play head for this too and move your play head to the point where you want your clip to end and then click on the button that says "out".

You can play around with your clip in your source monitor. Keep changing the position of your play head to select the most desirable "in" and "out" points and when you're done, just simply drag your video clip from your source monitor to the "new" button right below your project panel. This will create a new sequence for you containing the clip as well as a music file in it. To watch your sequence just click on it in the timeline and it will appear in the right top window named as "Cut only".

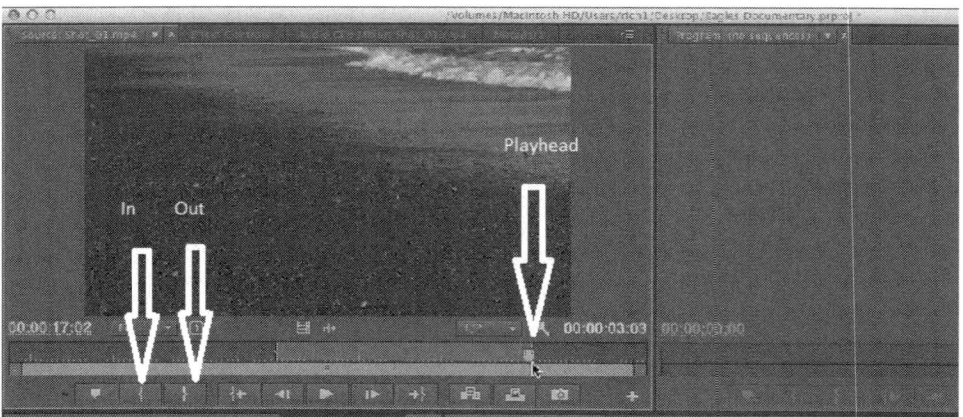

15 REMOVING AND ADDING AUDIO TO YOUR SEQUENCE

Sometimes the objective is to remove the audio track from your sequence. This can be done by simply going to your timeline window and selecting the music track while holding alt key to select the music track. Now press the delete key to remove your audio track from the sequence.☐

To add a new track to your sequence, simply open the bin in your project tab that contains your audio file and double click it. Now you will be able to see your audio file in your source monitor. You can do the same trimming on your audio files just like the way you did on your video files. When you're done with your trimming you can add your music file to your sequence by clicking on the overwrite button found in the tool bar just below your source monitor.

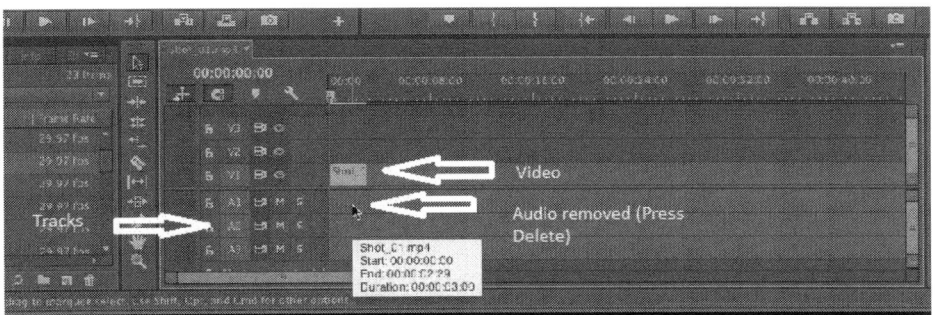

Don't forget to select the track on which you want to add your track on. You can do that by clicking on the track buttons inside your timeline window to highlight them. The highlighted track will upload the recent music file. You can also add multiple music files which is usually useful in making documentaries. To add another music file to your timeline repeat the same steps as you did for the first music file but before dropping your second file to your timeline make sure that you have selected a new track and deselected all others.

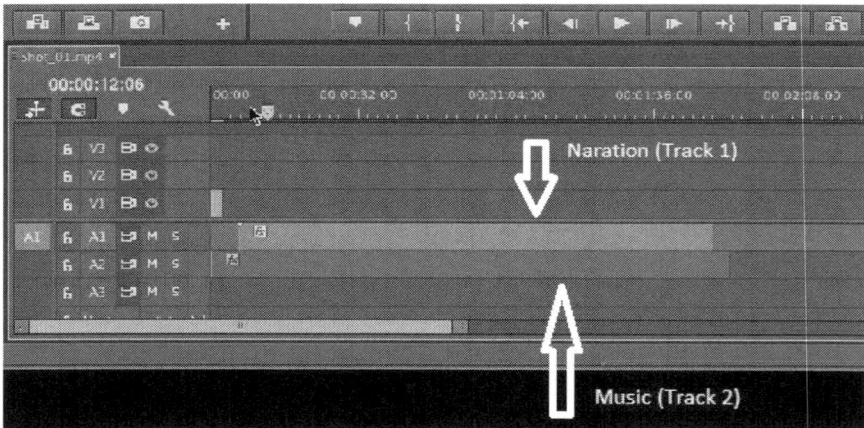

16 ADDING EFFECTS AND TRANSITIONS TO YOUR SEQUENCE

Most of the time there are lots of problems like color and light problems in our videos which will make our edited video a little bit dull. Adding effects to your timeline will make your new video much more professional and polished.

To add different kind of effects to your video first select the clip you want to add to effect to and then go to your effects panel found in the bottom left corner window. After selecting the effects panel you will be able to search and select different kinds of effects for your video. Just simply select the effect that you think is most suitable for your sequence and drag it over to your selected clip in timeline. If you can't find a specific effect then you can always use the search bar provided in the effects tab to search for a specific effect.

If you want to control or change the properties of a particular effect then simply go to your clip in the timeline and double click your clip. This will open your clip on the left top side of your screen and you can select the "effects control" tab to go to the properties of that effect. Here you can change all the properties like light, brightness etc. Of the added effect to get exactly what you want. Also, if you to add some transitioning effects than simply right click on the corner of a clip in your timeline and select default transitions from the menu. This will add a fading in or fading out transitioning effects on clip corners. □

You can add transitions to as many clips as you want and if you ever feel the need to add transitions to multiple clips then simply select all of them at once and go to the sequence option on the top of the screen and select apply default transition to selection from the drop down menu.

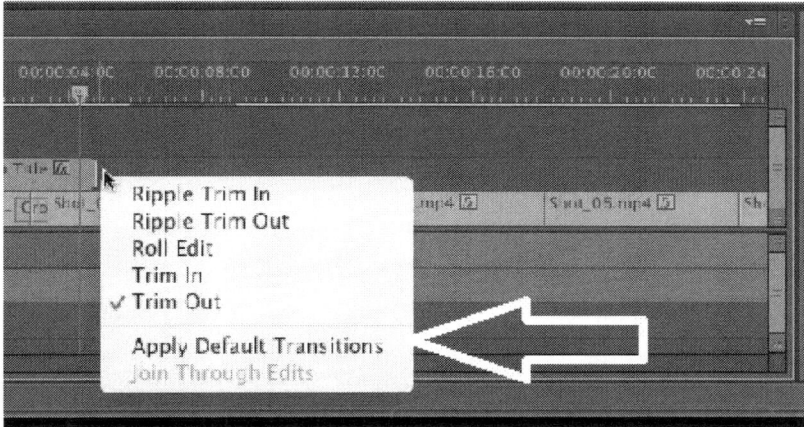

17 EXPORTING

Once you're done with your sequence and all of the editing, it's time to export your sequence so you can share it with others.

Exporting your edited file is a piece of cake. Just select all of your sequence or timeline clips and go to your File menu on the top left corner of your screen. From the drop down menu select Import and then Media. This will open a new exporting window for you where you can change several options according to your liking. Choose the format of your sequence (select H.264 if you're not familiar with the formats) and select the output name. Don't forget to change the option of your "Source Range" to "Entire sequence".

Now click on the export button to export your sequence.

In the previous chapter we discussed different ways of editing your video in Final Cut Pro (X) and here we did the same things in Adobe Premiere Pro.

18 TIME-LAPSE WITH GOPRO

Making a time-lapse video with your GoPro is one of the most fun things that you can do. Time-lapse, if you don't know, is a technique used by photographers to increase or decrease the speed of your videos.

Basically the idea behind time-lapse videos is to show an event like Sunset with an increased speed which would otherwise be really boring if you would have to sit and wait for a whole hour.

Usually time-lapse is done by taking a series of pictures after a specific interval of time and then combining them with an fps of your choice to make a video of the event. This way you are able to see an event, which would otherwise be really difficult to see, in a matter of minutes if not seconds. Consider the example of a construction of a huge building, a photographer will set its camera in front of the building and take pictures, let's say after every hour, for few days and then combine the pictures in one video so you can see the whole procedure of construction within a minute or two which in most cases is very enjoyable.

19 WHAT YOU'LL NEED FOR TIME-LAPSE

If you're a beginner you should be very careful in taking pictures for time-lapsing. It may seem an easy task but it's no child's play. You need to set your camera in a specific spot and possess the right equipment as well as set appropriate intervals in order for the time-lapse video to be amazing.

20 A STAND OR TRIPOD

The very first thing you'll need for taking pictures is a tripod. A tripod is an equipment or, in simple words, a stand for your camera. Time-lapse contains hundreds if not thousands of pictures and you can't take all of them by yourself. You need to set your camera at a comfortable spot from where you can get a good look at your subject. Make sure there's no obstacle between your camera and your subject.

21 SETTING THE INTERVALS

Usually you will need software or hardware like interval meter to set the time intervals between your pictures. But fortunately for you GoPro already provides a built-in interval setting function. Use that interval setting function to set an appropriate interval for your pictures. You should choose a longer interval for slower events for example an interval of a day would be appropriate for a growing plant. On the other hand an hour interval would be perfect to capture the movement of sun. So keep in mind the length of the event before setting the interval.

Also don't forget to charge your camera battery. Since your camera will be out there for a long period of time, it's wise to charge it to 100% otherwise you won't get the best of the event.

22 TIME-LAPSE IN FINAL CUT PRO

Making a time-lapse video in Final Cut Pro is really easy and straight forward. All you have to do is import your pictures (all of them) in your newly created project. Don't forget to make a new event when importing window appears.□

Once you're done importing your picture now simply select all your pictures and put them in your timeline window just like you do with other pictures, nothing special. Now go to your timeline and select all of your pictures in the timeline either by selecting all of them with your mouse or by pressing control + a. once you have selected all your pictures right click on them and select "New Compound Clip" from the popup menu. This will make a new clip from all your images.

Vlad Gemstone

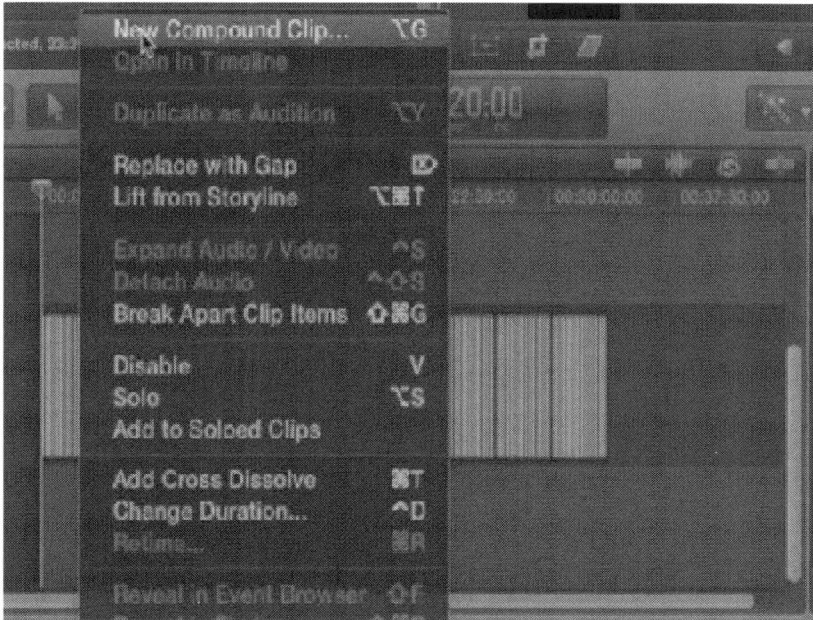

The newly created clip will be really slow and won't be fun to look at. You need to shorten the interval of each picture. Right click again on your timeline pictures and select "Retime" from the menu. A green bar will come at the top of your timeline pictures. Select and drag that green line to the left to shorten the frames of your time-lapse video. You can keep shortening until you're satisfied with the speed of the time-lapse video.

Once you're done with retiming your clip, your time-lapse video is ready. It's simple as that. Keep in mind that this is the basics of making a time-lapse in your final cut pro. There are lots of other things that you can do with your time-lapse video but if you're a beginner it would be wise to stick to basics.

23 TIME-LAPSE IN ADOBE PREMIERE

Making time-lapse videos in Adobe Premiere is easier if compared to Final Cut Pro. In Adobe Premiere all you have to do is import your pictures that you want to make time-lapse videos of, change some properties, if you want to, and that's it.

The first thing you need to do is to make a new project and a new sequence in your Adobe Premiere. Once you're done making your project now you need to import all your pictures so you can make a time-lapse video.

You can import videos either by going to Files > Import or select the files from "Media Browser" tab in the lower left corner of your Adobe Premiere screen. An important thing to keep in mind is to select the pictures carefully before importing.

If you simply select the pictures and import them then they will be imported as regular individual pictures. Since you are making a time-lapse video from those pictures you need to import them as a single clip. To do this, select the first picture and then check the "numbered stills" option and click ok. This will make sure that all your pictures come in a clip form rather than individual pictures.

Now that you have your pictures imported into your adobe premiere you can select them and change their properties or add effects like crop from the effects tab and do color corrections. You can do all the editing you want at this stage just as you would do with any other video file. Once your done editing all you have to do is go to files > export. Select the appropriate settings from the popped up window and export your clip.

24 CONCLUSION

These two video editing software's are the top editing tools out there on the market and the basics that this book covers will definitely make it really easy for you to edit or polish your GoPro videos on your own without having to spend some real cash on editing professionals. This was only an introductory book for people who didn't know anything about video editing, if you want to learn more then you can always use internet to browse through a series of photo editing software books.

See all of Vlad Gemstone

 Books, Foto and Bio

http://www.amazon.com/-/e/B00VTME5RW

Follow me on twitter @VladGemstone

Thank you very much both for downloading this eBook and for reading it from the beginning to the end.

If you enjoyed this book or found it useful

I'd be very grateful if you'd post a short review on Amazon.

Your post really does make a difference and I can get your feedback & make this book even better.

Vlad Gemstone

REFERENCES

Picture cover
©   <a
href="http://dreamstime.com/steveheap_info#res10301282">Steveheap<
/a> | <a
href="http://www.dreamstime.com/#res10301282">Dreamstime.com</
a> - <a href=" http://www.dreamstime.com/royalty-free-stock-image-
woman-cats-computer-desk-image22353936">Woman And Cats At
Computer Desk Photo</a>
href=" http://www.dreamstime.com/royalty-free-stock-image-romantic-
couple-young-beautiful-flower-sporty-bicycles-sunflowers-field-
background-image36282306</a>
License of use Picture -Web Usage (W-EL):
Electronic Items for Resale/Distribution: this license includes the right to
use the photos for webtemplates that are sold to more customers,
screensavers, e-cards, powerpoint presentations or as wallpapers on cell
phones. Maximum number of electronical items is 10,000 copies (applies as
a total of each type of usage). If this amount is exceeded you need to
acquire this license once again.
The new license will provide you with the standard amount of copies. This
is an additional license to the rights included within the regular Royalty-Free
license. Note that the other restrictions still apply.

20726667R00029

Printed in Poland
by Amazon Fulfillment
Poland Sp. z o.o., Wrocław